ABDELLATIF RAJI

Digital Outreach for Islamic Organizations

A Comprehensive Guide to Social Media, SEO, and Community Engagement

www.yarsak.com

Educational Use:

This book may be used for educational purposes by nonprofit organizations, educational institutions, and religious centers, provided that no part of this publication is reproduced, stored, or transmitted by any means for commercial purposes without the express permission of the author and publisher.

Accuracy of Information:

Every effort has been made to ensure the accuracy of the information provided in this book at the time of publication. However, the author and publisher make no representations or warranties regarding the completeness or accuracy of the information contained herein and shall not be liable for any errors, omissions, or damages arising from the use of this information.

Ethical Use of Content:

This book is intended to guide Islamic organizations in digital marketing in ways that align with ethical principles and Islamic values. Readers are encouraged to adapt the practices discussed in this book in a manner that is respectful and appropriate to their specific contexts.

Permission for Quotation:

Short excerpts from this book may be quoted for purposes of review, academic use, or media coverage, provided proper attribution to the author and title is given, and prior permission is obtained where necessary.

Limitation of Liability:

Neither the author nor the publisher shall be liable for any damages, direct or consequential, arising from the application or misuse of the concepts, strategies, or advice offered in this book. The responsibility for any action taken based on information in this book rests solely with the reader.

Changes in Information and Resources:

Due to the ever-evolving nature of digital platforms and resources, some content, URLs, or examples referenced in this book may change over time. Readers are encouraged to seek out the latest information and resources to ensure continued relevance and accuracy.

First edition

ISBN (paperback): 978-1-963876-87-1
ISBN (hardcover): 978-1-963876-83-3
ISBN (digital): 978-1-963876-86-4

This book was professionally typeset by Yaraak.
Find out more at yaraak.com

In the name of Allah, the Most Compassionate, the Most Merciful. This book is dedicated to all the leaders, volunteers, and members of Islamic organizations around the world who strive to make a positive impact in their communities every day. Your dedication to service, unity, and faith inspires change, uplifts lives, and brings light to those around you.

With gratitude and respect,
Abdellatif Raji

May this book guide Islamic organizations in harnessing the tools of today to uphold and spread the values of compassion, community, and integrity in service of humanity.

"And let there be [arising] from you a nation inviting to [all that is] good, enjoining what is right and forbidding what is wrong, and those will be the successful."

— SURAH AL-IMRAN, 3:104

Contents

Foreword

In recent years, Islamic organizations have seen a tremendous shift in the way they connect with their communities. Traditional avenues of outreach—such as Friday sermons, community gatherings, and charity events—remain essential, but digital platforms are now offering a transformative way to expand their mission, increase accessibility, and reach beyond geographical limitations. This book, **Digital Outreach for Islamic Organizations**, serves as a timely and much-needed resource for every Islamic leader, volunteer, and advocate who seeks to amplify their impact and remain connected in a digital age.

The journey of this book is rooted in the universal values of compassion, integrity, and community service. Every page reflects a deep respect for the values that guide Islamic organizations and aims to integrate these values seamlessly with modern digital marketing practices. In a world that often feels disconnected, this guide empowers Islamic organizations to build genuine connections, foster a sense of belonging, and provide much-needed support to people across the globe.

At its core, this book is not merely about adopting digital tools—it is about embracing a mindset that values ethical outreach, thoughtful engagement, and meaningful connection. The strategies presented here recognize that digital outreach must align with the principles of our faith. Through practical tips and insightful guidance, the author, Abdellatif Raji, has crafted a blueprint that allows Islamic organizations to maintain authenticity while thriving in the fast-paced, ever-evolving digital landscape.

Having witnessed firsthand the potential of digital outreach to inspire, uplift, and unify communities, I can attest to the relevance and importance of the insights within this book. For those unfamiliar with digital tools, this guide provides a solid foundation. For those already using them, it offers advanced strategies to refine and enhance their efforts. Each chapter is a call to action, urging organizations to adopt a proactive approach that honors tradition while embracing innovation.

As you delve into this book, may you be reminded of the profound impact Islamic organizations can have in the digital age. The tools of today, when used thoughtfully, can bridge divides, spread knowledge, and inspire positive change. With this guide in hand, may your organization continue to serve, uplift, and connect, embodying the principles that have guided Islamic communities for centuries.

— Syed Amjad Hussain Kamal
CEO IT & IS company and Founder & Principal

Preface

When I first began envisioning this book, I was struck by the unique challenges and opportunities Islamic organizations face in today's digital world. The need to stay connected with communities has never been more urgent, yet the ways in which we connect have evolved profoundly. Many organizations that serve the Muslim community—mosques, charities, educational institutions—operate with limited resources, relying heavily on the dedication of volunteers and the support of their local communities. Yet, with the rise of digital platforms, we now have tools to reach and inspire not just locally, but globally.

The goal of **Digital Outreach for Islamic Organizations** is to provide a practical guide that bridges the gap between traditional community-building efforts and modern digital marketing practices. This book was written with the understanding that digital marketing is not just about technology or strategy; it is about people. It is about building real, lasting connections that uphold the values of faith, integrity, and service that are at the heart of Islamic organizations.

In the following chapters, you will find insights on social media, email marketing, content creation, website optimization, and more. Each section is designed to help Islamic organizations of all sizes and stages of digital growth. Whether you're just beginning your digital journey or looking to refine your existing approach, this guide offers strategies tailored to the unique needs and goals of faith-based organizations.

Writing this book was a journey of discovery for me as well. I was inspired by the resilience, dedication, and compassion I've observed in the leaders and volunteers who give so much to their communities. This book is my way of contributing to those efforts, offering tools to empower organizations to serve, teach, and support on a larger scale. My hope is that it not only provides practical guidance but also serves as a source of encouragement and inspiration.

I am deeply grateful to the individuals and organizations who shared their insights and experiences with me during the creation of this book. Their stories and feedback have shaped its content and reminded me of the profound impact that Islamic organizations have on society. I extend my heartfelt thanks to everyone who supported this project and to the readers who embark on this journey.

May this book help your organization connect more meaningfully, serve more effectively, and bring benefit to communities both near and far. Insha'Allah, may it contribute to the greater purpose we all share: making the world a better place through acts of faith, compassion, and unity.

— Abdellatif Raji
10/24/2024

Acknowledgments

The journey of creating **Digital Outreach for Islamic Organizations** has been one of collaboration, learning, and inspiration. I am profoundly grateful to everyone who contributed their time, knowledge, and support in bringing this book to life.

First and foremost, I wish to thank the dedicated leaders, volunteers, and staff members of Islamic organizations who shared their insights, challenges, and successes with me. Your stories and experiences have deeply shaped the content of this book, and your commitment to serving your communities continues to be a source of inspiration.

A special thank you to my family and friends, whose encouragement and patience have been invaluable throughout this process. Your belief in this project has strengthened my resolve to see it through, and your support has been a constant source of motivation.

I would also like to extend my gratitude to the individuals and organizations who provided feedback on early drafts, offering valuable insights that helped shape the direction and clarity of this book. Your perspectives ensured that this work would be both practical and relevant for those who rely on it.

To the designers, editors, and publishing team, thank you for your expertise, guidance, and hard work. Your efforts behind the scenes have made this book possible, and I am grateful for your dedication to bringing this vision to life with professionalism and care.

Lastly, I am grateful to Allah for granting me the strength and inspiration to undertake this project. May this book serve as a means of benefit for Islamic organizations around the world, helping them reach new heights in their missions to educate, support, and unite.

Thank you to each and every one of you who played a role in this journey.

May your support and kindness be rewarded abundantly.

— Abdellatif Raji

10/24/2024

Prologue

In an era where digital communication has become integral to every part of life, Islamic organizations face unique opportunities and challenges. Traditionally, mosques, charities, and community centers have been cornerstones of support, guidance, and compassion within the Muslim community. But as society evolves, so too must these institutions, embracing new tools to continue their missions with resilience and purpose.

This book, **Digital Outreach for Islamic Organizations**, emerges from a vision to bridge centuries-old values with modern means of connection. As we enter a time where people are increasingly online, it's vital that Islamic organizations find their voice in this space, extending their reach to serve, educate, and inspire beyond geographical boundaries. Through digital marketing, social media, and other online channels, these institutions can amplify their messages of unity, compassion, and faith, engaging individuals who might otherwise be unreachable.

The journey to building a digital presence for an Islamic organization is not just about technology—it is about finding ways to connect authentically and uphold the mission with integrity. It requires understanding how to communicate Islamic teachings, engage with the community respectfully, and balance outreach efforts with the ethics and principles that define our faith. This book provides a roadmap for navigating this journey, drawing from proven digital strategies while staying aligned with the timeless values that guide our work.

Throughout these pages, you'll discover insights on social media, search engine optimization, content creation, email marketing, and more. Each chapter is crafted with the intention of empowering Islamic organizations to thrive in the digital space, offering practical advice grounded in ethical considerations and an awareness of the cultural nuances that shape our community.

As you embark on this path, remember that digital tools are extensions of the values and missions that your organization already embodies. They are a means to spread kindness, compassion, and support in a world that often needs it most. With this guide, may you find the inspiration and knowledge to forge meaningful digital connections, expand your impact, and continue the vital work of serving humanity in ways that align with the teachings of Islam.

Welcome to a journey of digital transformation, one that honors tradition while embracing the future.

— Abdellatif Raji
10/24/2024

Introduction

In today's digital era, the reach and influence of online platforms offer a unique opportunity for Islamic organizations to connect with a broader audience, promote their initiatives, and drive donations in ways that were previously unattainable. This book, **Digital Outreach for Islamic Organizations: A Comprehensive Guide to Social Media, SEO, and Community Engagement**, serves as a resource to help your organization establish an impactful and ethically responsible digital presence.

In a world where every organization, from small businesses to global nonprofits, leverages digital platforms to amplify their message, Islamic organizations must also adopt these tools to connect with their communities. With the help of digital marketing, mosques, charities, and community centers can broaden their outreach and cultivate a more engaged, informed, and supportive base of followers.

> "Digital marketing, when aligned with Islamic values, can become a powerful means of inspiring and connecting communities, providing real-time information, and enabling greater access to religious, educational, and charitable resources."

This guide will provide you with actionable strategies and insights to navigate the digital world, all while upholding the principles and values that are foundational to Islamic teachings. You will discover how to create authentic content, engage your community across various platforms, optimize your website, and measure your success to ensure continuous improvement.

Through carefully structured chapters, you'll delve into each aspect of digital marketing, beginning with building a strategy grounded in Islamic values. From there, we will explore the nuances of content creation, social media management, website optimization, email marketing, SEO, and digital advertising. Each chapter includes step-by-step guides, tailored tips, and examples that align with the ethos of Islamic organizations.

Whether you're a mosque, community center, or charity, this book is here to help you harness the potential of digital marketing to strengthen your connection with your community and maximize your impact.

Key Benefits of this Guide

- **Comprehensive Content:** Each chapter dives into core digital marketing areas with easy-to-follow steps and best practices.
- **Ethical Alignment:** Guidance on building a digital presence in a way that respects and honors Islamic values.
- **Community-Centric:** Tools and tips specifically tailored for the unique needs of Islamic organizations.

Let's begin our journey to understanding digital marketing from an Islamic perspective. In the upcoming chapters, you'll find in-depth information, examples, and practical exercises to help you apply each concept to your organization. With this guide, digital marketing becomes a means to strengthen your mission and further support your community.

1

CHAPTER 1: Building a Digital Strategy Aligned with Islamic Values

Understanding the Importance of a Digital Strategy

In a rapidly evolving digital landscape, Islamic organizations must develop a strategic approach to online engagement. A well-crafted digital strategy not only extends your reach but allows your organization to communicate in ways that resonate with and reflect the values of your community. The digital realm, after all, is more than just a platform for broadcasting; it's a space where communities are built, nurtured, and inspired. Therefore, designing a digital strategy that aligns with Islamic principles is essential for ensuring that your online presence genuinely reflects the integrity and mission of your organization.

Key Principles for Crafting an Effective and Values-Driven Digital Strategy

Your digital strategy should rest on pillars that serve as a framework for all online activities. These principles guide decision-making, content creation, and interactions, ensuring your digital marketing efforts remain consistent with Islamic values. Let's explore these pillars:

- **Authenticity:** Your message must be authentic and deeply rooted in the mission of your organization. In a world full of scripted messaging, honesty and genuine engagement will distinguish your organization.
- **Community-Centric:** Digital marketing for Islamic organizations should prioritize the needs and interests of the community. Understanding their values, concerns, and aspirations allows you to communicate effectively and offer meaningful support.
- **Ethical Integrity:** Islamic values prioritize ethical actions. Ensure transparency, avoid sensationalism, and prioritize messages that uphold your community's trust.
- **Educational Value:** Many online users are eager to learn. Focus on educating your audience, whether through Islamic teachings, community updates, or charitable initiatives.

Steps to Define and Implement Your Digital Strategy

Step 1: Define Your Mission and Vision

Begin by defining or refining your organization's mission and vision. These statements should encapsulate the purpose of your digital presence. Why does your organization need an online presence? How do you plan to benefit your community? By answering these questions, you will have a foundation upon which to build every component of your digital strategy.

"Your digital mission should echo your organization's core purpose, ensuring all online efforts are a true representation of your values and goals."

Step 2: Identify Your Audience and Their Needs

Who are you trying to reach? Every organization has a unique audience with distinct needs, values, and concerns. Conduct surveys, organize focus groups, and review engagement analytics to gain insights into your community. By understanding what resonates with them, you'll be better positioned to develop targeted content that speaks to their interests and supports your overall mission.

Step 3: Set Clear, Measurable Goals

Establishing clear goals is a crucial aspect of digital strategy. Determine specific objectives such as raising community awareness, increasing attendance at events, or boosting online donations. Goals should be measurable (e.g., grow social media followers by 20%) to track progress and make adjustments as needed.

Step 4: Choose the Right Platforms and Channels

Every social media and digital platform has its strengths. Facebook is excellent for community-building, Instagram for visually showcasing events, and YouTube for sharing educational videos. Choose platforms that align with your goals and audience. Avoid overwhelming your team by focusing on 2-3 channels that will best serve your objectives.

Step 5: Plan Your Content and Engagement Strategy

Develop a content calendar that reflects Islamic values and promotes your organization's mission. Balance between educational content, event promotions, community highlights, and donation drives. Be consistent, but also flexible, allowing room for timely posts that respond to relevant issues or celebrations within the Islamic calendar.

Executing Your Strategy with Continuous Improvement

A digital strategy should not be static. Regularly monitor and evaluate the performance of your digital initiatives through metrics such as engagement rates, website traffic, and feedback from your community. Adjust your approach as necessary to ensure continuous alignment with both your goals and Islamic values.

Your digital strategy is more than a collection of online activities; it is a cohesive plan that, when followed consistently, can transform your organization's reach and impact. With a strong, values-driven digital strategy, your organization will not only grow its online presence but also cultivate a meaningful, lasting connection with your community.

2

CHAPTER 2: Crafting Content That Resonates with Your Audience

The Power of Content in Building Community

Content is at the heart of every digital marketing strategy, particularly for Islamic organizations aiming to foster a sense of community and inspire action. Crafting content that speaks to the needs, values, and concerns of your audience strengthens connections, builds trust, and allows your organization to stay relevant in the lives of your followers. However, for content to resonate deeply, it must be authentic, educational, and culturally sensitive—especially in a religious context. In this chapter, we'll explore strategies to create impactful content that embodies these values.

Identifying Content Themes that Reflect Islamic Values

When planning your content, it's crucial to select themes that align with Islamic teachings and resonate with your community's needs. Some of the most impactful themes for Islamic organizations include:

- **Educational Content:** Share teachings from the Quran and Hadith, explore the significance of Islamic holidays, or provide guidance on Islamic practices.

- **Community Stories:** Highlight the achievements of community members, showcase events, and celebrate successes to build a sense of unity and pride.
- **Charitable Initiatives:** Share stories of charitable work and encourage donations by showing the real-life impact of contributions.
- **Events and Programs:** Promote upcoming events and programs, providing all necessary details to boost attendance and engagement.

Aligning content themes with your audience's interests creates a strong foundation for meaningful engagement. Remember, your audience may range from young Muslims exploring their faith to established community members looking to deepen their understanding and involvement. Tailor content that speaks to all segments to foster inclusivity.

Steps to Craft Effective and Engaging Content

Step 1: Define the Purpose of Each Content Piece

Each piece of content should have a specific purpose, whether it's to inform, inspire, educate, or drive action. For example, a social media post announcing a new program might aim to attract attendees, while a video about Ramadan could be designed to educate viewers on fasting practices. Defining the purpose ensures each post serves a role in your overall digital strategy.

> "Purpose-driven content serves as a guiding light, ensuring that every piece you create contributes to a larger narrative that resonates with your community."

Step 2: Use Authentic Language and Tone

Language matters, especially when addressing topics of faith and community. Use language that is respectful, clear, and free from jargon. Your tone should reflect the warmth and respect that is foundational to Islamic communication. If your organization uses Quranic verses or Hadith, always verify translations to maintain accuracy and respect.

Step 3: Balance Between Visual and Text Content

Visual content, such as images and videos, often attracts more attention than text alone. Use high-quality visuals that are appropriate and culturally sensitive. For instance, share images from recent community events, or create infographics to illustrate Islamic concepts. Ensure that all visuals align with Islamic principles, showing respect and modesty, and that they enhance, rather than detract from, the message.

Step 4: Engage Through Stories and Personal Narratives

People are naturally drawn to stories, especially those that they can relate to on a personal level. Share stories from your community members, highlight the journeys of those who benefit from your charitable work, or recount inspiring historical events from Islamic history. These narratives not only engage but also inspire empathy and solidarity within your audience.

Tailoring Content for Different Platforms

Not all content performs equally across platforms. Adjusting your approach for each platform ensures maximum engagement. Here's a breakdown:

- **Facebook:** Ideal for community updates, event promotions, and interactive content like Q&As. Share content that encourages likes, shares, and comments.

- **Instagram:** Perfect for sharing visually appealing content like event photos, quotes, and infographics. Use stories to engage followers with behind-the-scenes glimpses of your work.
- **YouTube:** Suitable for longer educational videos, event recordings, and in-depth tutorials. This platform is excellent for reaching those who prefer video content over written material.
- **Email Newsletters:** Provide in-depth content, monthly updates, and exclusive insights. Emails can foster a more personal connection and allow for longer-form content.

Crafting a Content Calendar for Consistency and Engagement

To maintain a consistent online presence, develop a content calendar. This schedule should outline content themes, post timings, and target platforms. A content calendar not only keeps you organized but also allows you to plan content around Islamic events and holidays, ensuring timely and relevant posts.

Tips for a Strong Content Calendar:

- Plan content around significant dates, like Ramadan, Eid, or community events.
- Incorporate a mix of content types to keep the audience engaged (e.g., images, videos, educational posts).
- Schedule regular posts to maintain a consistent online presence, balancing educational content with community updates.

In Summary

Creating content that resonates with your audience is about more than just posting on social media. It's about delivering messages that educate, inspire, and engage, while also reflecting the values and mission of your organization. By carefully selecting content themes, using authentic language, and tailoring posts to specific platforms, your Islamic organization can develop a content strategy that fosters connection and inspires action.

Through effective content, your organization can become not only a source of information but also a trusted and beloved part of your community's daily life.

3

CHAPTER 3: Social Media Marketing: Engaging Your Community

Why Social Media Matters for Islamic Organizations

Social media has become a powerful tool for reaching and engaging communities, offering Islamic organizations a unique platform to inspire, educate, and build a strong support network. Through Facebook, Instagram, Twitter, and other platforms, your organization can connect directly with its audience, promote events, share Islamic teachings, and highlight community activities. But achieving meaningful engagement requires more than just regular posting—it demands a thoughtful strategy that is sensitive to Islamic values and responsive to the community's needs.

Choosing the Right Social Media Platforms

Not all social media platforms are created equal, and each has its strengths when it comes to reaching different segments of your audience. Choosing the right platforms is essential for maximizing your reach and ensuring that your message is seen by the people it's intended for.

- **Facebook:** Ideal for community-building and sharing a variety of content types, including events, news, and long-form posts. With its groups and event features, Facebook enables a close-knit, interactive experience that can bring your community together.
- **Instagram:** Best suited for visually engaging content, such as photos and videos from community events or inspirational quotes. Instagram is popular among younger audiences and can help humanize your organization by showcasing the people and stories behind your work.
- **Twitter:** A platform for quick updates, news, and real-time engagement. Use Twitter to share important announcements or participate in trending discussions relevant to the community.
- **YouTube:** An excellent platform for longer educational videos, live streams of events, or tutorials. YouTube can help your organization create a repository of resources that can be revisited anytime.

Creating a Social Media Content Strategy

Step 1: Define Your Goals and Objectives

Each post on social media should serve a purpose, whether it's to raise awareness, engage your community, or inspire action. Clearly defining your goals and objectives for social media helps streamline your content creation and ensures each post aligns with your broader mission. For example, if your goal is to increase event attendance, focus on posts that highlight upcoming events and encourage RSVPs.

Step 2: Develop Content Pillars

Content pillars are recurring themes or topics that guide the types of posts you'll share on social media. For Islamic organizations, common content pillars may include:

- **Educational Content:** Share teachings, reminders, or quotes from the

Quran and Hadith.

- **Community Engagement:** Promote events, share stories, and recognize members' contributions.
- **Charitable Initiatives:** Highlight ongoing projects and showcase the impact of donations.
- **Inspirational Messages:** Post motivational quotes and reflections to uplift and inspire your audience.

Organizing your content around these pillars ensures consistency, making it easier for your audience to engage with and understand your organization's mission.

Step 3: Create a Posting Schedule

Consistency is key to building an engaged social media community. Create a posting schedule that reflects the frequency and times when your audience is most active. For instance, posting before or after prayer times might yield higher engagement among your followers. Plan for regular posts each week but remain flexible to accommodate important or timely updates.

Engaging Your Audience with Interactive Content

Engagement goes beyond likes and shares; it's about creating a dialogue with your audience. Interactive content allows followers to become active participants in your online community, making them feel valued and heard.

- **Polls and Q&A Sessions:** Host polls to gather opinions or conduct Q&A sessions on topics of interest. This not only encourages engagement but provides insight into your audience's views.
- **Live Streams:** Use live streaming to share events, conduct webinars, or deliver Friday messages. Live videos add a personal touch, fostering a stronger sense of connection.
- **Comments and Replies:** Respond to comments on your posts. Engage

in conversations with your followers by addressing questions, acknowledging feedback, and offering words of encouragement.

Managing and Growing Your Social Media Presence

Step 1: Monitor Engagement Metrics

Track key metrics such as likes, shares, comments, and follower growth to assess the impact of your social media efforts. Reviewing these metrics helps you understand which types of content resonate best with your audience, allowing you to refine your strategy over time.

Step 2: Collaborate with Influencers and Partners

Consider collaborating with influencers, local leaders, or partner organizations who share your values. Such partnerships can expand your reach and introduce your organization to new audiences. Choose collaborators who genuinely align with your mission to maintain the integrity of your brand.

Step 3: Use Hashtags to Increase Discoverability

Hashtags can boost the visibility of your posts and connect you with a wider audience. For Islamic organizations, hashtags like #IslamicRelief, #Ramadan, #Charity, and others relevant to your content can make it easier for interested users to find your posts. However, avoid overusing hashtags—select a few targeted ones for maximum impact.

In Summary

Social media provides Islamic organizations with unparalleled opportunities to connect, educate, and inspire their communities. By selecting the right platforms, creating engaging content, and maintaining an interactive presence, your organization can become a valuable resource and a beloved part of your community's digital life. As you grow your social media presence, remember to always prioritize authenticity, consistency, and respect for your audience's values.

Through strategic social media marketing, your organization can foster a vibrant online community and broaden its positive impact within and beyond the local area.

4

CHAPTER 4: Optimizing Your Website for Increased Visibility

The Role of Your Website in Digital Outreach

Y our website is the digital hub of your organization, acting as a central location for information, resources, and updates. For Islamic organizations, a well-optimized website can increase visibility, making it easier for community members and potential donors to connect with your initiatives, access educational content, and stay informed about upcoming events. A highly visible website extends your reach and reinforces the credibility of your organization, enhancing its impact.

Understanding SEO and Why It Matters

Search engine optimization (SEO) is the practice of improving your website so it ranks higher in search engine results. This increased visibility makes it more likely that people searching for Islamic resources, community events, or charity opportunities will find your website. Optimizing your site for search engines isn't just a technical task; it's a way of making your content accessible to those who need it. Effective SEO strategies bring your valuable work to a broader audience.

Key Components of SEO for Islamic Organizations

SEO involves a mix of on-page and off-page strategies that improve your website's search engine ranking. Let's explore the core components of SEO, each of which can contribute to making your site more visible and accessible to the community.

1. Keyword Research

Keywords are the terms people use to find information online. Conduct keyword research to identify relevant words and phrases that people might use when searching for content related to Islamic teachings, community events, or charitable activities. Use tools like Google's Keyword Planner or other SEO tools to discover high-traffic keywords such as "Islamic charity," "Ramadan donations," or "mosque events."

Tip: Focus on long-tail keywords—phrases that are more specific, like "Islamic charity for orphans" or "Friday prayer times in [Your City]." These are often less competitive and can attract a more targeted audience.

2. On-Page Optimization

On-page optimization refers to optimizing individual pages on your website to improve their search engine rankings. This includes using keywords in strategic places such as:

- **Title Tags:** The title tag should include the main keyword and clearly describe the page's content.
- **Headings:** Use your primary keywords in headings (H1, H2, H3) to help search engines understand the page's structure and content.
- **Meta Descriptions:** A brief summary of the page's content. Make it compelling and include relevant keywords.

- **Alt Text for Images:** Search engines can't read images, so use alt text to describe them and include keywords where appropriate.

By placing keywords naturally throughout your content, you increase the likelihood that search engines will recognize and rank your pages for those terms.

3. Quality Content Creation

Quality content is fundamental to SEO. Creating educational and engaging content that meets your audience's needs keeps them on your site longer, signaling to search engines that your website is valuable. Regularly update your website with blog posts, guides, or event announcements that offer insights into Islamic teachings, community initiatives, or charity work.

    Example: Publish a blog post on the importance of giving during Ramadan, or a guide to the benefits of community gatherings in Islam. Such content provides value to visitors and encourages them to explore other areas of your website.

4. Mobile Optimization

With more users accessing websites on their mobile devices, mobile optimization is crucial. A responsive design ensures your website looks good and functions well on smartphones and tablets. Search engines like Google prioritize mobile-friendly sites, so make sure your content is easily readable on smaller screens and that all features are fully functional.

    Tip: Test your website on multiple devices to ensure a seamless experience for mobile users. Mobile-friendly sites tend to rank higher and provide a better user experience.

5. Page Speed Optimization

Page speed is a critical SEO factor. A slow website frustrates users, causing them to leave, which negatively affects your rankings. Use tools like Google PageSpeed Insights to analyze and improve your website's load times. Simple adjustments like compressing images, enabling browser caching, and minimizing CSS and JavaScript can significantly improve speed.

Building Backlinks for Authority and Credibility

Backlinks are links from other websites to yours, and they signal to search engines that your website is trustworthy and valuable. Building backlinks from reputable sites can improve your search ranking. Reach out to community partners, collaborate with Islamic bloggers, or get listed in online directories to increase your site's backlinks.

Example: If your organization is involved in a charity project, ask partner organizations or local news outlets to link to your website in their coverage. Backlinks from high-quality sites boost your website's credibility.

Tracking Your SEO Progress

Regularly monitor your SEO performance to understand what's working and where there's room for improvement. Use tools like Google Analytics to track metrics such as page views, bounce rates, and traffic sources. Keep an eye on keyword rankings to see how your pages are performing in search results. By tracking these metrics, you can refine your SEO strategy over time.

Tip: Set up Google Search Console to monitor any technical issues that might affect your site's visibility and receive recommendations on improving SEO.

In Summary

Optimizing your website for search engines is a powerful way to extend the reach of your Islamic organization and ensure that your message reaches those seeking information, community, and support. By focusing on keywords, quality content, mobile optimization, page speed, and building backlinks, your website will rank higher and attract more visitors. A strong online presence amplifies your organization's mission and allows you to serve your community more effectively.

With a well-optimized website, your organization is poised to make a greater impact, share valuable resources, and provide a welcoming digital space for those interested in learning more about your work.

5

CHAPTER 5: Email Campaigns: Staying Connected with Your Supporters

Why Email Marketing is Essential for Islamic Organizations

E mail marketing remains one of the most effective digital channels for nurturing and strengthening relationships with supporters. For Islamic organizations, email campaigns offer a direct, personalized way to communicate important messages, share updates, and inspire action among your audience. Unlike social media, email allows you to maintain control over your audience engagement, ensuring your community stays connected with your organization without the limitations of algorithms.

Building Your Email Subscriber List

A well-curated email list is foundational to a successful campaign. Building a list of engaged subscribers starts with making it easy and appealing for people to sign up. Use multiple methods to encourage sign-ups, such as:

- **Website Signup Forms:** Place a signup form on your website's homepage, blog, and contact page to capture visitors who are interested in receiving updates.

- **Event Registrations:** Encourage people who register for events to join your email list to receive follow-up information and news on upcoming programs.
- **Social Media Prompts:** Use social media to invite followers to subscribe for exclusive content or updates on upcoming activities and charitable initiatives.
- **In-Person Events:** Collect email addresses at events by offering a quick and easy signup option, such as a tablet at the welcome table.

Tip: Clearly communicate the benefits of subscribing, such as receiving early event notifications, educational content, or updates on charitable projects.

Crafting Effective Email Content that Resonates

1. Personalize Your Emails

Personalized emails are more likely to engage recipients. Use subscribers' first names in greetings, segment your list to cater to specific interests, and tailor content based on previous interactions. For instance, those who have donated in the past might appreciate updates on how their contributions are making a difference, while volunteers may want information on upcoming service opportunities.

> "Personalization shows your community members that they are valued, helping to build a stronger connection and increase engagement."

2. Use Compelling Subject Lines

Your subject line is the first thing recipients see and plays a major role in determining whether they'll open your email. Aim for clear, concise, and intriguing subject lines that communicate the value of opening the email.

25

Examples include:

- "Join Us in Making a Difference This Ramadan"
- "New Event This Friday: Don't Miss Out!"
- "Your Monthly Update: Community News & Upcoming Programs"

Keep subject lines under 50 characters to ensure they're fully visible on mobile devices.

3. Offer Valuable and Relevant Content

Your audience subscribes to your emails because they believe your content will provide value. Consistently deliver on this expectation by including updates, educational insights, event information, and inspiring stories. Examples of content that can engage and inform include:

- **Upcoming Events:** Share details about prayer meetings, lectures, community iftars, and other events, with RSVP links for easy sign-up.
- **Charity Updates:** Provide updates on ongoing projects, showcase impact stories, and highlight ways to contribute.
- **Educational Resources:** Send short reflections, links to Islamic teachings, or articles on topics that matter to your community.

Example: Consider creating a monthly newsletter with a mix of community news, inspiring content, and practical resources.

Designing Your Emails for Maximum Impact

1. Keep Layout Simple and Visual

A clean, simple layout makes your emails easy to read and navigate. Include images from recent events, but avoid overloading the email with visuals that may distract from the main message. Use clear headings, bullet points, and white space to enhance readability.

2. Use Clear Calls-to-Action (CTAs)

Guide readers to take action by using clear, compelling CTAs, such as "Join Us," "Donate Now," or "Learn More." Place CTAs prominently in the email and make sure they are easy to click on mobile devices. CTAs should align with the main goal of your email, whether it's to increase event attendance or gather donations.

3. Optimize for Mobile

With many users checking emails on mobile devices, ensure your emails are mobile-friendly. Use a responsive design that adjusts to different screen sizes, and test emails on both desktop and mobile to confirm they display correctly.

Creating an Effective Email Campaign Schedule

A well-planned email campaign schedule helps you stay organized and maintain a consistent presence in your subscribers' inboxes. Plan your emails around important events and dates in the Islamic calendar, such as Ramadan, Eid, and local community events.

Suggested Frequency: Aim to send 1-2 emails per month, ensuring each one provides valuable content. Increase the frequency during key periods like Ramadan when engagement tends to be higher, and subscribers are more inclined to support charitable causes.

Tracking and Improving Your Email Campaigns

Analyzing your email campaign performance provides insights into what resonates with your audience and allows you to continually improve your approach. Track key metrics such as:

- **Open Rates:** Percentage of subscribers who open the email. High open rates indicate engaging subject lines and relevant content.
- **Click-Through Rates (CTR):** Percentage of recipients who click on links within the email. Higher CTRs suggest your CTAs are effective and the content is engaging.
- **Unsubscribe Rate:** Keep an eye on this rate to ensure your content remains relevant and engaging for your audience.

Use these insights to refine your content, timing, and design, ensuring your email campaigns continue to deliver value to your community.

In Summary

Email marketing offers a powerful channel for Islamic organizations to keep their communities informed, inspired, and connected. Through well-crafted emails, personalized content, and a consistent campaign schedule, your organization can nurture relationships, drive engagement, and encourage ongoing support. By providing relevant and meaningful content, you'll create an email program that not only informs but also strengthens the sense of community and purpose within your organization.

6

CHAPTER 6: Search Engine Optimization (SEO) for Islamic Organizations

Understanding the Role of SEO in Reaching a Wider Audience

For Islamic organizations aiming to expand their reach and impact, SEO plays a critical role in attracting a wider audience. By optimizing your website to rank higher on search engine results pages, you make it easier for people seeking information, resources, or a community to discover your organization online. With effective SEO, your website can become a trusted resource, reaching those who might not yet know about your work but are interested in learning more or getting involved.

Step 1: Conducting Keyword Research to Connect with Your Audience

Keyword research is the foundation of SEO. Start by identifying phrases your target audience might use when searching for information or resources related to Islamic teachings, events, or charitable initiatives. Using these keywords strategically on your site helps search engines connect your content to relevant user queries.

- **Tools for Keyword Research:** Use tools like Google Keyword Planner, Ahrefs, or SEMrush to identify popular and relevant keywords.
- **Examples of Keywords:** Examples might include "Islamic charity," "Eid events near me," or "Friday prayer times in [Your City]." Focus on both broad terms and specific, long-tail keywords for better targeting.

Tip: Prioritize keywords with moderate to high search volume and low competition to reach users effectively.

Step 2: On-Page SEO to Enhance Your Website's Relevance

Optimizing Titles and Headings

Your website's title tags and headings (H1, H2, etc.) should include your target keywords. These elements are crucial for helping search engines understand the content of each page and for guiding users to relevant information.

    Example: For a page about Ramadan, use a title tag like "Understanding Ramadan: Significance, Practices, and Community Events" to capture both the topic and relevant keywords.

Writing Compelling Meta Descriptions

A meta description is a brief summary that appears in search results below your page title. Use this space to describe your content compellingly, including relevant keywords to increase click-through rates.

Example: "Learn about the importance of Ramadan, upcoming community events, and ways to give back during this blessed month. Join our organization's mission to spread unity and knowledge."

Using Alt Text for Images

Alt text is a short description of an image, which improves accessibility and helps search engines interpret the content of the image. Use keywords where relevant but ensure the description accurately reflects the image.

Step 3: Creating High-Quality Content to Attract and Retain Visitors

Content is king when it comes to SEO. High-quality, informative, and relevant content not only engages your audience but also signals to search engines that your website is a valuable resource. Consider producing content that addresses common questions, provides educational insights, or highlights community events.

- **Educational Blog Posts:** Write posts on topics such as "The Significance of Zakat" or "The Benefits of Friday Prayer in Islam."
- **Resource Guides:** Create comprehensive guides on Islamic teachings or a "What to Expect" guide for newcomers attending mosque events.
- **Event Highlights:** Publish summaries of recent events, complete with photos and key takeaways, to create engaging content that captures your organization's activity.

Step 4: Improving Website Usability and Mobile-Friendliness

A website that is easy to navigate and optimized for mobile devices performs better in search engine rankings. Most users will visit your site from a mobile device, so ensuring a responsive design that adjusts to all screen sizes is essential.

Tip: Test your site's mobile-friendliness using Google's Mobile-Friendly Test tool to identify areas for improvement.

Step 5: Building Backlinks to Strengthen Your Site's Authority

Backlinks—links from other reputable websites to yours—are a powerful factor in SEO. They signal to search engines that other trusted sites consider your content valuable, boosting your credibility. Reach out to other Islamic organizations, local news outlets, or religious bloggers for link-building opportunities.

Example: Collaborate on community projects and ask partner organizations to include a link to your website in their event announcements or recaps.

Tracking and Refining Your SEO Efforts

Monitor your SEO performance using tools like Google Analytics and Google Search Console to track page views, bounce rates, and keyword rankings. Regularly review these metrics to understand what's working and make necessary adjustments to improve your site's performance.

- **Adjust Content Based on Popular Keywords:** Analyze which pages perform best and consider updating underperforming pages with more relevant keywords or improved content.
- **Fix Technical SEO Issues:** Use Search Console to identify issues like broken links, slow-loading pages, or mobile usability errors that can negatively impact your rankings.

In Summary

SEO is an ongoing process that requires consistent effort and refinement, but the payoff can be significant for Islamic organizations. By optimizing your website with keywords, creating valuable content, improving usability, and building backlinks, you increase your site's visibility and attract a larger, engaged audience. This expanded reach allows you to share your mission more widely and connect with individuals interested in supporting or joining your organization.

With a well-executed SEO strategy, your website can become a central resource, drawing people to your cause and establishing your organization as a beacon of knowledge and community in the digital space.

CHAPTER 7: Promoting Events and Initiatives Online

The Importance of Online Event Promotion for Islamic Organizations

Event promotion is a crucial aspect of community-building for Islamic organizations. Whether you're organizing a prayer gathering, charity fundraiser, educational seminar, or holiday celebration, effective online promotion can help you reach a wider audience, encourage attendance, and create excitement. Promoting events online allows you to reach not only local community members but also individuals who may wish to attend virtually or support the initiative from afar.

Step 1: Define Your Event Goals and Target Audience

Start by defining the purpose of your event and identifying the audience you wish to reach. Are you aiming to raise funds, increase awareness, or build community engagement? Your goals will shape your promotional strategy. Additionally, understanding your audience—whether it's young adults, families, or senior community members—helps you tailor your messaging and select the most effective channels for outreach.

Example: For a Ramadan fundraiser, your target audience may include community members, local businesses, and potential online donors. Your messaging could focus on the spiritual rewards of giving during Ramadan and the tangible impact of their contributions.

Step 2: Leverage Social Media to Build Awareness

Create Event Pages on Facebook and Instagram

Facebook and Instagram provide specific features for event promotion. Use Facebook's event creation tool to outline the event's details, including date, location, description, and RSVP options. Encourage attendees to invite their friends and share the event, increasing reach within their networks.

Instagram doesn't have an event feature, but you can promote events through regular posts, stories, and highlights. Use engaging visuals, countdown stickers, and hashtags to build excitement and remind followers as the event date approaches.

Use Hashtags to Increase Discoverability

Hashtags can make your event posts more discoverable to a broader audience. Consider using general hashtags related to Islamic events (e.g., #Ramadan2023, #IslamicCharity), as well as specific ones for your organization (e.g., #[YourOrganization]Event). This strategy helps people find your posts and stay informed.

Step 3: Send Targeted Email Invitations and Reminders

Email marketing remains one of the most effective ways to reach your existing community. Create personalized email invitations that detail the event's purpose, location, date, and RSVP instructions. Follow up with reminders as the event date nears, using these emails to build anticipation and highlight any new updates, guest speakers, or special activities.

Tip: Segment your email list if possible, targeting different groups with customized messages. For example, you could send one version to potential donors focusing on the impact of their support and another version to general attendees with event highlights.

Step 4: Use Your Website as a Central Information Hub

Your website is an ideal location for providing comprehensive information about the event. Create a dedicated event page with all essential details, including RSVP options, donation links, and a schedule if applicable. Include a clear call-to-action (CTA) for attendees, such as "Register Now" or "Donate to Support the Event."

If your event is recurring, consider maintaining a calendar of upcoming events to keep your community informed year-round.

Step 5: Collaborate with Community Partners and Influencers

Partnering with local businesses, community leaders, and influencers can help expand your event's reach. Identify community figures or organizations with an audience that aligns with your mission. Encourage them to promote the event on their social media or include it in their newsletters.

Example: Partner with a popular local restaurant to offer iftar for a Ramadan event, and ask them to promote the event through their social media platforms to attract additional attendees.

Step 6: Create Engaging Visual Content

Visual content is essential for capturing attention and encouraging people to attend or support your event. Use images, videos, and graphics that reflect the spirit of the event. For example, create a video invitation from key speakers, a countdown graphic, or an infographic detailing how funds raised will be used.

Tip: Consistent branding, including colors, fonts, and logos, across all promotional materials, helps reinforce your organization's identity and creates a cohesive look.

Step 7: Engage Attendees Before, During, and After the Event

Before the Event: Build Anticipation

In the days leading up to the event, keep the excitement going by sharing teasers, behind-the-scenes content, and reminders. Use stories and posts to highlight guest speakers, special activities, or the importance of attending. Personalize reminders for attendees who have RSVP'd, showing appreciation for their commitment.

During the Event: Use Live Updates

Engage your online audience by sharing live updates during the event. Use Instagram and Facebook Live to broadcast portions of the event, such as speeches or prayer sessions. This allows those who couldn't attend in person to participate virtually and enhances the reach of your event.

After the Event: Follow-Up with Attendees

After the event, send a thank-you email to attendees, expressing gratitude for their participation and summarizing the event's impact. Share event highlights on social media and your website, including photos, videos, and key takeaways. Encourage those who couldn't attend to watch recordings or get involved in future events.

Tip: Use post-event engagement to build momentum for your next event. Provide a link to upcoming events or donation opportunities to keep your audience engaged.

In Summary

Promoting events and initiatives online helps Islamic organizations reach a broader audience, foster community involvement, and achieve event goals. By leveraging social media, email, your website, and community partnerships, you can create a multi-channel promotion strategy that maximizes attendance and engagement. Engaging your community throughout the event journey—from pre-event anticipation to post-event follow-up—ensures a memorable experience that strengthens your organization's connection with its supporters.

With effective online event promotion, your organization can create events that resonate, inspire, and build a strong, connected community.

8

CHAPTER 8: Utilizing Digital Advertising within an Ethical Framework

The Role of Digital Advertising for Islamic Organizations

D igital advertising can be a powerful tool to help Islamic organizations increase their visibility, attract donations, and encourage community involvement. While organic reach is valuable, advertisements allow you to target specific audiences, reach new supporters, and boost attendance for events and campaigns. However, to align with Islamic principles, it is essential to approach digital advertising with an ethical framework that respects and upholds the values of transparency, modesty, and integrity.

Setting Clear Objectives for Digital Advertising

Before launching any digital advertising campaign, clearly define your objectives. This ensures that your ads are purpose-driven and allows you to allocate resources effectively. Common goals for Islamic organizations might include:

- **Increasing Donations:** Create ads that highlight specific charitable initiatives or showcase the impact of past contributions.
- **Promoting Events:** Use ads to spread awareness about upcoming events, such as community gatherings, fundraisers, or educational seminars.
- **Building Brand Awareness:** Ads can introduce your organization to new audiences, particularly those outside of your immediate community.

Example: An ad campaign for Ramadan donations could feature stories and images of individuals benefiting from the organization's work, providing a tangible connection between donor contributions and community impact.

Selecting the Right Platforms for Your Ads

Choosing the right advertising platform is key to reaching your target audience. Consider which platforms align with your objectives and where your audience is most active. Common platforms for digital advertising include:

- **Facebook and Instagram:** Ideal for community engagement and event promotion, with options for precise audience targeting based on location, interests, and demographics.
- **Google Ads:** Great for reaching people actively searching for related content. Use Google's search and display network to attract users looking for Islamic resources, charity opportunities, or local events.
- **YouTube Ads:** If your organization produces video content, YouTube ads can expand your reach. Use engaging videos to tell your organization's story or explain a campaign's impact.

Crafting Ethically Aligned and Engaging Ad Content

Use Transparent and Respectful Messaging

Transparency in advertising is essential for building trust and honoring Islamic values. Clearly explain the purpose of each ad, avoid exaggerated claims, and ensure that the content reflects the integrity of your organization.

Example: Instead of making bold claims about fundraising goals, an ad could emphasize community-driven impact, showing how contributions help real people in need.

Focus on Storytelling to Engage Emotionally

Storytelling is a powerful method for connecting with audiences on a deeper level. Share stories that highlight the lives touched by your organization's work, demonstrating the positive impact of their support.

Example: Use video or carousel ads to tell a series of stories about individuals who have benefited from your organization's programs, each image or video representing a chapter in the story.

Ensure Modesty in Visual Content

Choose visuals that are respectful and modest, reflecting Islamic principles. This approach not only maintains the dignity of those featured but also aligns with the expectations of your audience.

Tip: Use high-quality, professional images that respectfully depict community members, volunteers, or beneficiaries.

Targeting Your Audience Thoughtfully and Responsibly

Digital platforms allow precise targeting based on demographics, interests, behaviors, and geographic location. Use these tools thoughtfully to reach the right audience without over-targeting or invading privacy. For Islamic organizations, it's crucial to select targeting criteria that ensure ads are relevant, useful, and aligned with your ethical standards.

Example: For a campaign promoting local charity events, target users within a specific geographic area rather than casting a wide net, ensuring your ad reaches individuals most likely to attend.

Measuring and Analyzing Ad Performance

Tracking your ad performance allows you to see which strategies are most effective and helps you optimize future campaigns. Focus on key metrics such as click-through rate (CTR), conversion rate, and cost per conversion. These insights guide adjustments to improve effectiveness and ROI.

- **Click-Through Rate (CTR):** A high CTR indicates that your audience finds your ad compelling and relevant.
- **Conversion Rate:** This metric reveals how many people take the desired action, such as donating or signing up for an event, after clicking on your ad.
- **Cost Per Conversion:** This helps you understand the financial efficiency of your ads, ensuring a good return on investment.

Regularly review and refine your ads based on performance data to maximize impact and align spending with your organization's budget and goals.

In Summary

Digital advertising offers Islamic organizations a valuable tool for expanding their reach, increasing support, and achieving meaningful goals. By approaching advertising with a clear ethical framework—focusing on transparency, respectful visuals, and responsible targeting—your organization can use ads to enhance its digital presence while staying true to Islamic values. Tracking performance metrics ensures you continually improve and optimize your strategy, maximizing your organization's impact while maintaining integrity.

With well-crafted digital advertising campaigns, your organization can effectively connect with its audience, inspire action, and foster a sense of community and shared purpose.

9

CHAPTER 9: Driving Donations Through Online Channels

The Growing Importance of Online Donations for Islamic Organizations

For Islamic organizations, online donations are essential for sustaining charitable initiatives, community programs, and day-to-day operations. As more people turn to digital platforms for their giving, it's crucial to provide convenient and secure online donation options. By leveraging online channels effectively, you can reach a broader audience, increase donation amounts, and drive consistent support for your organization's mission.

Building a Donation-Friendly Website

1. Create a Clear and Accessible Donation Page

Your donation page should be easy to find, simple to navigate, and mobile-friendly. Include a prominent "Donate" button on your homepage and in the website's header so visitors can quickly access it. Use straightforward language and clearly outline where donations go and how they make an impact.

Example: "Your contribution helps provide essential resources for families in need, fund educational programs, and support our community events."

2. Offer Multiple Payment Options

To accommodate a wide range of donors, provide various payment options such as credit cards, bank transfers, and platforms like PayPal. Additionally, consider enabling options for recurring donations, allowing supporters to set up monthly contributions easily.

Using Social Media to Encourage Donations

Social media is a powerful tool for reaching potential donors and encouraging them to support your organization. Share stories, images, and videos that demonstrate the impact of donations, and include links to your donation page to simplify the giving process.

1. Create a Campaign with a Clear Call to Action

A focused campaign with a clear call to action increases the likelihood of receiving donations. For instance, during Ramadan, you might launch a "Ramadan Giving" campaign with messages that emphasize the rewards of charity during this blessed time. Encourage supporters to share the campaign to reach an even larger audience.

2. Use Visual Content to Inspire Generosity

Visuals play a vital role in emotionally engaging your audience. Use compelling images and videos that highlight the people or projects benefiting from donations. Real stories from those your organization has helped create a powerful connection, encouraging supporters to contribute.

Enhancing Email Campaigns for Fundraising

Email marketing is an excellent channel for fundraising, as it allows you to share detailed information about your campaigns and directly ask for support. Craft personalized, impactful messages that remind recipients of the importance of their contributions.

1. Personalize Your Email Appeals

Address donors by name and, if possible, refer to their past contributions to create a personalized experience. Thank them for their ongoing support and illustrate how their generosity has made a difference in your organization's work.

2. Provide Clear Links to Donation Options

Make it easy for recipients to donate by including prominent buttons or links in the email. Use strong calls to action like "Support Our Cause Today" or "Make a Lasting Impact" to encourage donations. Ensure that the donation process is simple and seamless.

Creating Urgency with Limited-Time Campaigns

Creating a sense of urgency can motivate supporters to act quickly. Limited-time campaigns, such as year-end fundraising drives or Ramadan campaigns, encourage donors to make a contribution within a specific timeframe. Clearly communicate the importance of immediate action in your messaging.

Example: "This Ramadan, help us reach our goal of providing meals for 500 families. Donate today and be part of a meaningful change."

Acknowledging and Retaining Donors

1. Show Appreciation to Your Donors

Acknowledging donors shows that you value their support and encourages them to continue contributing in the future. Send thank-you emails, include donors in your organization's newsletter, or even highlight donors in social media posts if appropriate.

2. Provide Updates on How Donations are Used

Keep donors engaged by updating them on how their contributions have been used. Share stories, photos, or videos of completed projects or testimonials from those who have benefited. This transparency builds trust and strengthens the relationship between your organization and its supporters.

In Summary

Online donations are an indispensable source of support for Islamic organizations, enabling them to continue and expand their work. By creating a user-friendly donation page, leveraging social media, utilizing email campaigns, and fostering urgency, you can inspire your community to give generously. Showing appreciation and providing transparent updates keep donors engaged and loyal, ensuring sustained support for your mission.

With a thoughtful approach to online fundraising, your organization can thrive and make a greater impact within the community, fostering a culture of generosity and collective purpose.

CHAPTER 10: Measuring Success and Adapting Your Strategy

The Importance of Tracking and Measuring Digital Success

For Islamic organizations, the success of digital marketing efforts isn't solely based on reach but on meaningful engagement and impact within the community. Measuring the effectiveness of your digital strategy provides insights into what resonates with your audience and helps identify areas for improvement. Through careful tracking, you can adapt your approach to better serve your organization's mission, increase engagement, and make more informed decisions about future campaigns.

Key Metrics to Track for Each Digital Channel

Different digital channels have unique metrics that can indicate success or areas that need adjustment. Here's a breakdown of key metrics to monitor across platforms:

- **Website Analytics:** Track page views, average time spent on page, bounce rate, and conversion rate (e.g., donations or sign-ups).

- **Social Media Metrics:** Monitor engagement (likes, shares, comments), reach, follower growth, and clicks on links shared.
- **Email Marketing:** Focus on open rate, click-through rate (CTR), conversion rate, and unsubscribe rate to gauge engagement with your emails.
- **Online Donations:** Track total donation amount, number of donors, and average donation size to assess fundraising efforts.

Tip: Use Google Analytics, social media insights, and email marketing platforms to access and analyze these metrics.

Evaluating the Impact of Content

Content is a significant part of any digital strategy. Evaluating how your content performs allows you to refine messaging and formats to better engage your audience. Assess the types of posts, articles, or videos that attract the most attention and those that inspire action.

1. Identify Top-Performing Content

Determine which pieces of content received the most engagement by reviewing metrics such as shares, likes, comments, and time spent on page. For example, if inspirational posts or educational videos receive higher engagement, consider creating more content in these formats.

2. Track Content Conversion Rates

Conversion rate measures how well your content encourages users to take a desired action, such as signing up for an event or making a donation. Analyzing which content leads to conversions helps you understand what types of messages and formats are most effective.

Adjusting Your Digital Strategy Based on Insights

1. Refine Audience Targeting

Analyzing demographic and behavior data can reveal new opportunities to target your audience more precisely. For example, if younger followers respond more to Instagram content, while older audiences engage with email newsletters, adjust your strategy to focus content accordingly on each platform.

2. Optimize Timing and Frequency of Posts

Data from social media and email platforms can show when your audience is most active, helping you schedule posts and emails for maximum visibility. Experiment with posting times and frequency, and track results to find the best schedule for your organization.

3. A/B Test Campaign Elements

A/B testing involves creating two variations of a campaign element—such as an email subject line, ad image, or CTA button—to see which performs better. By continuously testing elements and analyzing results, you can refine each aspect of your digital strategy to improve outcomes.

Setting and Reviewing Key Performance Indicators (KPIs)

KPIs are specific metrics that measure progress toward your organization's goals. Set achievable KPIs for each area of your digital strategy to monitor overall performance. Examples might include increasing website traffic by 20%, growing social media followers by 10%, or raising $5,000 in online donations over three months.

Tip: Review your KPIs quarterly or annually to evaluate progress and make necessary adjustments to stay aligned with your organization's mission and goals.

Encouraging Team Collaboration and Continuous Improvement

Digital marketing is an evolving field, and success requires a collaborative effort. Encourage team members to share insights from their areas and hold regular strategy review meetings. This allows your organization to learn from successes and challenges, continuously improve, and keep your strategy fresh and effective.

Example: Have team members from social media, content creation, and fundraising meet monthly to discuss campaign performance, share feedback, and brainstorm new ideas for engaging the community.

In Summary

Measuring and adapting your digital strategy is essential for sustained success. By tracking key metrics, evaluating content impact, refining audience targeting, and fostering collaboration, your organization can make data-driven decisions that enhance your digital presence and maximize community impact. With a commitment to continuous improvement, your organization can create a lasting and meaningful connection with supporters and fulfill its mission more effectively.

Through strategic measurement and adjustment, your digital marketing efforts will remain dynamic and responsive, empowering your Islamic organization to thrive and grow in the digital space.

11

CHAPTER 11: Building a Sustainable Digital Presence for Long-Term Impact

The Importance of a Long-Term Digital Strategy for Islamic Organizations

For Islamic organizations, a sustainable digital presence is key to achieving lasting impact, engaging the community continuously, and adapting to changing digital landscapes. Unlike short-term campaigns, a long-term strategy allows your organization to build trust, strengthen relationships, and foster an enduring online community. This chapter explores essential strategies for creating a digital presence that can grow, evolve, and remain impactful over time.

Establishing a Consistent Brand Identity Across Digital Platforms

Consistency in branding across all digital channels reinforces your organization's mission and makes it easily recognizable. A clear, unified brand identity reflects professionalism, builds trust, and keeps your audience engaged.

1. Develop Core Branding Elements

Core branding elements include your logo, color scheme, fonts, and voice. Each should reflect the values of your organization and resonate with your audience. When your visual and verbal messaging are consistent, it strengthens your online presence and makes your organization memorable.

2. Apply Branding Consistently Across Channels

Use your branding elements consistently on social media, your website, email newsletters, and other platforms. Ensure that your logo, colors, and messaging style align on every platform, from social media posts to blog articles and event invitations.

Fostering Community Engagement and Loyalty

Building a digital community requires more than just posting updates—it's about actively engaging and interacting with your audience. By nurturing relationships online, your organization can create a loyal following that supports your mission year-round.

1. Prioritize Interaction and Responsiveness

Engagement builds trust and shows that you value your audience's input. Reply to comments, answer questions, and show appreciation for supporters on social media and email. This two-way communication strengthens the sense of community and fosters loyalty.

2. Host Regular Online Events and Webinars

Virtual events such as webinars, live Q&A sessions, or online workshops can attract a wide audience, including those who may not attend in-person events. These events offer valuable learning opportunities and give followers a sense of belonging, enhancing community ties.

Creating Content that Remains Relevant Over Time

Evergreen content—content that stays relevant long-term—provides lasting value to your audience and helps attract consistent web traffic. Balance your digital content strategy between timely posts (such as event announcements) and evergreen topics.

1. Focus on Educational and Resourceful Content

Create content that educates and provides resources, such as guides to Islamic practices, charity FAQs, or introductory articles on your organization's mission. This type of content remains relevant and serves as a reference for new followers over time.

2. Update Existing Content Regularly

Review your top-performing content periodically to ensure it remains accurate and up-to-date. For example, an article on Ramadan giving tips might need updating with new donation options or updated dates each year.

Investing in Team Training and Skill Development

A sustainable digital strategy requires a skilled team. By investing in training and skill development, your organization can stay ahead of digital trends and improve the effectiveness of your outreach.

1. Train Team Members in Digital Marketing Skills

Ensure your team has the skills necessary for digital marketing success, such as social media management, content creation, SEO, and data analysis. Training can be conducted through workshops, online courses, or mentorship programs.

2. Encourage Collaboration and Innovation

Foster a collaborative environment where team members can share insights, brainstorm ideas, and experiment with new strategies. Regular team meetings can promote open communication, helping your organization adapt to changes more smoothly.

Planning for Scalability and Future Growth

As your organization's digital presence grows, it's important to plan for scalability. This involves setting up processes, tools, and strategies that allow your organization to expand without compromising quality or consistency.

1. Use Scalable Digital Tools

Adopt tools that can grow with your organization, such as CRM software for donor management, scheduling tools for social media, and analytics platforms for tracking performance. Scalable tools reduce manual effort, allowing your team to focus on high-impact work.

2. Develop a Long-Term Content and Campaign Calendar

A long-term content calendar helps ensure consistent messaging and allows you to plan around major events, Islamic holidays, and annual fundraising drives. By scheduling campaigns in advance, your organization can maintain a steady online presence year-round.

In Summary

Building a sustainable digital presence is essential for Islamic organizations that want to foster long-term community engagement and adapt to an ever-evolving digital environment. By establishing a consistent brand identity, creating engaging content, investing in team skills, and planning for growth, your organization can create a resilient digital strategy that will serve its mission for years to come. This sustained approach empowers your organization to make a lasting impact, expand its reach, and strengthen connections within the community.

With a commitment to a sustainable and forward-thinking digital presence, your organization is well-positioned to navigate future challenges, embrace new opportunities, and continue its vital work in serving and uplifting the community.

12

CHAPTER 12: Additional Resources and Practical Tools for Islamic Organizations

Digital Tools to Enhance Your Organization's Strategy

As your organization moves forward with its digital strategy, several tools can streamline operations, improve engagement, and maximize your outreach efforts. Below is a curated list of practical tools, each with a specific function to help your organization thrive in the digital space.

- **Social Media Management:** Tools like **Hootsuite** and **Buffer** allow you to schedule posts, track engagement metrics, and manage multiple social media accounts from a single dashboard.
- **Email Marketing:** Platforms like **Mailchimp** and **Constant Contact** provide robust email templates, segmentation tools, and automation features to keep your supporters informed and engaged.
- **Website Analytics: Google Analytics** is essential for tracking website traffic, understanding audience behavior, and identifying high-performing pages.
- **Keyword Research and SEO:** Tools such as **Google Keyword Planner**

and **Ahrefs** assist with keyword research and SEO optimization, helping your website rank higher in search results.

- **Donation Platforms:** Solutions like **GiveWP** and **PayPal Donations** offer secure and customizable donation options directly on your website.
- **Content Creation: Canva** is a versatile design tool perfect for creating visually engaging social media graphics, posters, and newsletters tailored to your organization's branding.

Further Reading and Educational Resources

For those interested in exploring more about digital marketing, community engagement, and nonprofit growth, consider these recommended resources:

- **Books:**
- *Jab, Jab, Jab, Right Hook* by Gary Vaynerchuk – A guide to effective social media storytelling and content creation.
- *The Art of Social Media* by Guy Kawasaki and Peg Fitzpatrick – A practical resource on building and managing a successful social media presence.
- *Nonprofit Fundraising 101* by Darian Rodriguez Heyman – Comprehensive advice on fundraising strategies, including online approaches.
- **Websites and Blogs:**
- **Nonprofit Tech for Good:** Offers valuable insights on digital marketing, social media, and fundraising for nonprofit organizations.
- **Mashable Social Good:** Features articles and trends on how nonprofits can use digital platforms to drive impact.
- **HubSpot Blog:** A rich resource for articles on SEO, content marketing, social media, and more.

Workshops and Courses

Consider enrolling in online courses or attending workshops that deepen your understanding of digital marketing and community building. Here are some recommended platforms:

- **Google's Digital Garage:** Free courses on topics like digital marketing, SEO, and analytics.
- **Coursera:** Offers comprehensive courses from top universities on nonprofit management, social media strategy, and content marketing.
- **Udemy:** Courses on digital marketing basics, social media management, and donor engagement designed for nonprofits.
- **HubSpot Academy:** Free certification courses covering digital marketing, social media, and SEO fundamentals.

Staying Inspired and Connected

The world of digital marketing is constantly evolving, and staying inspired is essential to keeping your strategy fresh and effective. Join online communities, participate in webinars, and subscribe to newsletters that offer industry insights. Engaging with a network of like-minded organizations and professionals can provide inspiration and practical advice to help your organization continuously improve.

Example: Consider joining groups on LinkedIn focused on nonprofit marketing, Islamic organizations, or community outreach to exchange ideas, ask questions, and learn from the experiences of others.

Final Words: Continuing the Journey with Confidence

Embracing digital marketing and outreach allows your Islamic organization to connect more deeply with the community, extend its impact, and stay resilient in a dynamic world. By building skills, using the right tools, and staying true to your values, your organization can thrive online and continue fulfilling its vital mission.

May this guide serve as a foundation for your journey in digital outreach, inspiring meaningful connections and growth. Your work is valuable, and each digital interaction, post, and campaign holds the potential to make a positive, lasting difference in the lives of many.

13

Conclusion

Empowering Islamic Organizations Through Digital Marketing

As Islamic organizations continue to embrace the digital world, the potential to connect with communities, spread valuable knowledge, and drive impactful change has never been greater. This guide, **Digital Outreach for Islamic Organizations: A Comprehensive Guide to Social Media, SEO, and Community Engagement**, offers a pathway for mosques, charities, and community centers to navigate the online landscape with purpose, integrity, and effectiveness.

Reflecting on the Power of Digital Marketing Aligned with Islamic Values

The power of digital marketing lies not only in its reach but in its ability to foster genuine relationships and drive meaningful action. By grounding your digital strategy in Islamic values—such as integrity, community focus, and ethical engagement—your organization can create an online presence that is both impactful and true to its mission. Each chapter in this guide emphasizes how to implement digital strategies that not only engage audiences but do so in a way that respects and upholds the principles of Islamic teachings.

Achieving Impact Through Consistent and Authentic Engagement

An authentic, engaging, and consistent approach is key to fostering long-lasting connections with your community. Through well-curated content, strategic use of social media, engaging email campaigns, and a well-optimized website, your organization can build a trustworthy and accessible online presence. Authenticity in every message and action allows your audience to feel seen, valued, and inspired to support your mission.

Adapting and Growing in a Dynamic Digital Landscape

The digital landscape is continuously evolving, and Islamic organizations must remain adaptable to harness new tools and trends effectively. By regularly measuring success, analyzing performance, and adjusting strategies, your organization can remain relevant and impactful. Training your team in new skills and investing in scalable tools and systems prepares your organization for sustainable growth, allowing you to expand your reach and impact over time.

The Road Ahead: Continuing the Mission Online and Offline

With a comprehensive digital strategy, your organization can reach people across the world, share Islamic teachings, promote charity and social justice, and foster a strong, supportive community. However, digital outreach is a complement to, not a replacement for, the invaluable work your organization does in person. Together, your online and offline efforts can empower your community, inspire action, and deepen connections.

> "May your digital journey be one that enhances your organization's mission, brings people together, and spreads the message of unity, compassion, and generosity."

As you move forward, remember that every post, email, and interaction is an opportunity to make a difference, share knowledge, and inspire support. With dedication, ethical practices, and an unwavering commitment to Islamic values, your organization can make a profound impact through digital means, empowering a global community to come together in shared purpose.

Thank you for embarking on this journey. May your organization's digital presence continue to be a source of guidance, connection, and inspiration for years to come.

Epilogue

As we reach the end of **Digital Outreach for Islamic Organizations**, it is my hope that this book serves not only as a guide but as a source of inspiration for all who seek to make a difference through their work. The journey of bringing an organization's mission to the digital realm is one filled with both challenges and rewards. In every post, campaign, and connection lies the potential to spread messages of unity, compassion, and hope, echoing the timeless values that form the foundation of our communities.

The digital age offers us tools and platforms that transcend borders, allowing Islamic organizations to reach individuals who may have once been out of reach. This is a unique opportunity—an unprecedented chance to share knowledge, provide support, and nurture connections on a global scale. But with this power comes a responsibility to use these tools thoughtfully, ethically, and with integrity.

As you move forward, remember that digital outreach is not about numbers or trends; it is about creating a meaningful impact. Every interaction online, no matter how small, is an opportunity to reflect the values of our faith and to invite others to experience the beauty of community, charity, and mutual respect. In the words of the Prophet Muhammad (ﷺ), "The best of people are those that bring the most benefit to the rest of mankind." May this principle guide each effort, reminding us that true success lies in service and in bringing light to others.

Thank you for allowing this book to be part of your journey. May your organization continue to grow, inspire, and serve with purpose. And may the work you do online and offline leave a lasting legacy of kindness, wisdom, and unity for generations to come.

— Abdellatif Raji

Afterword

Writing **Digital Outreach for Islamic Organizations** has been a journey of both reflection and discovery. It has reinforced my belief that Islamic organizations hold immense potential to shape communities, nurture understanding, and provide guidance in a world that often feels increasingly complex and fast-paced. The digital world is vast and, at times, daunting. Yet, within it lies an unparalleled opportunity for outreach, growth, and connection—opportunities that, if harnessed with care, can bring countless benefits to our communities.

This book is the product of countless conversations, reflections, and observations gathered over the years. From speaking with leaders of Islamic organizations to understanding the needs of the communities they serve, each experience highlighted the importance of being present, accessible, and genuine in every form of outreach. The digital landscape may seem impersonal, but it is the intention behind each effort that brings warmth, sincerity, and meaning to this space.

As we move forward, I am reminded of the importance of staying adaptable and open to learning. Digital platforms will continue to evolve, and new tools will emerge. Yet, our core mission—to uplift, serve, and educate—will remain timeless. I encourage all readers and organizations to embrace both the old and the new, to remember the values that define us, and to be bold in exploring the possibilities the digital world offers.

May this book serve as a stepping stone, a resource that you can revisit and adapt as your organization grows. It has been my sincere honor to walk this path with you through these pages, and I hope the knowledge shared here empowers you to make a meaningful impact, connect deeply with your communities, and spread messages of unity, compassion, and purpose far and wide.

Thank you for taking this journey with me, and may your efforts in the digital world continue to shine a light on the values that matter most.

— Abdellatif Raji
10/24/2024

About the Author

Abdellatif Raji is a dedicated advocate for community-building, with a passion for empowering Islamic organizations to harness the potential of digital platforms. With a background in digital marketing and years of experience working with faith-based nonprofits, Abdellatif has witnessed firsthand the transformative power of strategic outreach in fostering meaningful connections and inspiring action.

Abdellatif's work bridges traditional values with modern technology, focusing on approaches that allow organizations to grow their reach, deepen engagement, and remain true to the principles of Islam. Throughout his career, he has provided consulting and support to various mosques, charities, and Islamic centers, guiding them in effectively using social media, email marketing, SEO, and other tools to fulfill their missions.

His goal in writing **Digital Outreach for Islamic Organizations** is to share this knowledge and offer a practical guide for organizations that are ready to embrace digital opportunities while staying aligned with their ethical and spiritual foundations. Abdellatif believes that by using technology thoughtfully, Islamic organizations can make a profound impact on their communities, inspiring greater unity, compassion, and understanding in a world that needs it more than ever.

When he is not working on digital outreach projects or writing, Abdellatif enjoys studying Islamic history, exploring new technology trends, and spending time with his family. He is committed to lifelong learning and is always looking for ways to support the growth and success of organizations working for positive change.

For inquiries, speaking engagements, or consulting, you can reach Abdellatif at contact@abdellatifraji.com.

You can connect with me on:

🌐 https://yaraak.com

𝕏 https://x.com/yaraak_agency

📘 https://www.facebook.com/yaraak.agency

Subscribe to my newsletter:

✉ https://abdellatifraji.com

www.ingramcontent.com/pod-product-compliance
Lightning Source LLC
Chambersburg PA
CBHW071031280326
41935CB00011B/1538